Finding Your Worth in Christ

Identifying Your Worth through the Lens of Your Creator

Joele S. Leith

WESTBOW
PRESS®
A DIVISION OF THOMAS NELSON
& ZONDERVAN

WestBow Press books may be ordered through booksellers or by contacting:

WestBow Press
A Division of Thomas Nelson & Zondervan
1663 Liberty Drive
Bloomington, IN 47403
www.westbowpress.com
844-714-3454

Scripture quotations taken from The Holy Bible, New International
Version® NIV® Copyright © 1973 1978 1984 2011 by Biblica, Inc.
TM. Used by permission. All rights reserved worldwide.

ISBN: 978-1-6642-1127-8 (sc)
ISBN: 978-1-6642-1126-1 (e)

Library of Congress Control Number: 2020921651

Print information available on the last page.

WestBow Press rev. date: 11/30/2020

Contents

Acknowledgment

I began writing my testimony to someday share my journey of discovering who I was through Christ. The manuscript took over four years to compose, and it required listening to what the Lord had me write. I honor those who helped me.

God the Father and Holy Spirit, whose words spoken through me enabled me to write.

David Leith, my soul mate, support for life, and leader of our home. I could not have done this without him.

Jon Leith, for telling me, "You have to do this, Mom," when I didn't think I could.

Jade Leith, for teaching me to have faith in this process and for constantly encouraging me.

Jennifer Leith, for being a living support throughout my spiritual journey to being ordained and becoming a leader for God. She always guided and instructed me to see things in a larger perspective.

 To my immediate family, for giving me a work ethic and encouraging me to never quit. They instilled God in my life and were always in my corner.

Chapter One

My Story—Growing Up and Being Saved

WHEN I WAS YOUNGER, I WATCHED MY GRANDMOTHER create the most beautiful quilts. She created stacks of colorful material all with two-by-two squares. There must have been hundreds of them. I was too young to really understand just how important each piece was and how detailed quilting by hand really was.

Each piece matters and is well thought out in terms of how it attaches to the next in the same way God pieces your story together. Did you know that you were intricately woven and well thought out in your mother's womb and that you have a purpose beyond just existing? Psalm 139:13 says, "You created my inmost being; you knit me together in my mother's womb." I hope that through my story, God will give you a glimpse of how you are uniquely created for more. He is bringing truth about where your identity comes from in and through Christ.

I am the firstborn child and have one sister. Growing up, we always had a lot of love in our family. My father is from France and my mother is American, and we were blessed to have all our essential needs met. I had a special connection to my grandparents, who brought a lot of comfort and peace in my life. They were role models for how God intends a family unit to be, and they set the tone for what I wanted my family to eventually look like.

Even though I had the basic needs in my life, I remember as a child and into my young adult years, feeling I was missing something. I felt very empty in many ways. I now know that there was so much more God needed to show me before I would be ready and equipped to walk out the purpose I was called to do on this earth and who I was to become.

God needed to build my understanding of who I was and where my identity came from. For my entire life, I knew God was there, and I had seen faith in action modeled for me by my mother. But it wasn't until I sought God out for a personal relationship and surrendered my life fully to the Lord that I had a true revelation of who God really was and how He loved and cared for me. It was that moment that Christ set me free to live the life He had designed and called me for.

In July 2000, I stood in complete curiosity and confusion in a room filled with women who were huddled in a circle and deep in prayer at a Mary Kay women's convention. The feeling in the room that evening was electric, powerful. I had no idea how their prayer time was so different from mine all through the twenty-five years of my life of prayer. I had prayed most of my life, and my mother had instilled values in me that helped me grow the relationship I had with the Lord, but I felt so alone and empty. *How could these women possibly feel so alive and on fire?* I wondered. *Where is this energy coming from? Why haven't I ever experienced it? How can I get what they have?*

I asked one of my coworkers to fill me in on what I was missing, and she led me to the Lord and prayed the prayer of salvation over me. I obediently repeated the words that would change my life forever. I asked the Lord into my heart and surrendered my life that day and declared that I needed a savior, Jesus Christ, and that He was the only way to the Father.

That was only the beginning of my story of what God had in store for me. The angels rejoiced in heaven that day, but I was clueless as to how to take my next steps. John 3:16 says, "For God so loved the world that he gave his one and only Son, that whoever believes in him shall not perish by have eternal life." John 14:6 says, "Jesus answered, 'I am the way and the truth and the life. No one comes to the Father except through me.'"

Prior to this moment, I was heading down a dead-end path to find what I thought was true joy and love. I was trying desperately to find my hope and love through men. I was trying to control my life and create a safe environment in which I could feel complete. Unfortunately, dating and putting my trust in others turned out to be a dead end. I was unsatisfied, broken, and shame filled; I felt unworthy of love or anything else. I longed for earthly things that just continued to disappoint me.

During my teenage years, I saw a change in my dad, who struggled with many things from his past. As a result, we were not able to experience the fullness of love God intended a daughter to receive from a father. We can give to others only what we possess. He did the best he could as a parent, but that made it hard for me to feel loved by anyone. I found ways to cope and please my own needs, and I put up a wall around my heart because I didn't know what else to do.

I poured my energy into friends, drinking, relationships, and really anything else that could keep me busy and give me some sense of relief from my emotional pain. I had a mixed understanding that my successes and accomplishments would equal my worth. I believed if I just did more, became more, performed more, and perfected myself and my life that I would finally feel whole. After years upon years of doing life my way, I hit a wall. A huge wall. I was at the end of my rope and my efforts and could not keep up anymore with the only way I knew how to be.

There are moments that change our lives in one of two ways—either we choose to continue on our path leading to physical and spiritual death or we realize we need a savior and can't do life on our own.

After surrendering my life to God, it was not all easy. It was far from perfect. But it was the beginning of a transformation. I was eager to learn all I could; I got involved in a few good Bible studies and began to skim through the Bible. In my childhood, I attended a traditional church and went to Sunday school classes each week, but I still did not know the love of God or the Bible.

In the first five or six years, I struggled fitting in as a new believer. I was plugged into a very large church that really began to lead me to profess my faith in public. I chose to be baptized, which I believe was the start of my activating more of what God had for me. I was full of emotions, and I desired to go deeper and get to know God on a more intimate level.

Then God began to reveal things to me. I didn't doubt He was talking directly to me. He began to tell me things about people and show me visions of people and situations to pray for. I began to feel others' pain at times as though it were my own, and I knew I needed to find people who could mentor me and help me understand what was happening.

My prayers were answered when I met a woman who would change my life. I began taking classes at the Arise School of the Supernatural Ministry, which was the first-year course at the Bethel School of Supernatural Ministry out of Redding, California. Pastor Debbie Greenlee purchased the course from Bethel and began teaching in Mishawaka, Indiana.

For the next two years, God began to do a great work in and through me. I began to listen and actually hear Him more clearly than ever. I was in an environment that encouraged my special gifts and taught me to pray and release instead of internalize all the painful things I was praying about or feeling for others.

I realized that my first assignment was to intercede in prayer for people. God began to show me things on a whole new level, and I was drawing near to all He had for me. During my time in the school, we learned how to be still, pray, and listen to what the Holy Spirit wanted to teach us. We went on spiritual treasure hunts to strengthen our abilities to hear who needed prayer. We would leave the church, go where God directed us, and find those He needed us to pray over.

I was blown away while doing these spiritual treasure hunts. I heard from God about the struggles people were going through and what to pray for, and I had visions of what to look for—someone in a certain color shirt or doing something specific. Once, I had a vision of a yellow coat and received a clue about a right arm. Then I found a woman testing her blood pressure with her right arm in the monitor and wearing the yellow coat I had seen.

When approaching the many people God had spoken to me about, those on the receiving end always had God encounters in that they were experiences that pointed directly to God's orchestrating a stranger such as myself to know the exact things they needed help and prayer for.

While in the school, I learned that my self-worth and giftings were in the Lord and that my purpose was huge. I learned to share God's Word with the people He had me share with and to set my fears aside. I began not to worry about how others would perceive me more and more, and I focused totally on being a vessel for God. I was finally feeling a purpose beyond any earthly accomplishment or major milestone I had experienced. He began to talk to me through visions, feelings, smells, and words of knowledge. This opened my world up to the greatest change I would ever experience.

The Holy Spirit was working in me and was being birthed and revealed (which I will discuss more in chapter 2). I have had many encounters with others during which I have been able to feel what they were feeling. I had to learn to ask God, "Who is the person needing prayer?" For example, one time, I felt a slight pain in my shoulder just before walking into a restaurant to have lunch with a friend, who began complaining about her shoulder. I prayed aloud asking God to rid this pain in the name of Jesus. I received this word of knowledge, and her pain never returned. That happened a number of times since then, and I can now distinguish between my own pain that is real and the pain of someone in need of prayer.

I have also experienced visions of whom to pray for. One time, I was at the sink washing a Pyrex dish; water was flowing onto the back of the dish, and I saw the imprint of a child's hand as the water separated when hitting the glass. That startled me, and I asked God, "What does this mean? How am I to pray specifically?" I heard that I was to pray for the soul of a child, so I did. Later, I heard on the news that a tragic car accident had claimed the lives of some children.

I learned to be obedient in prayer and to carry specific words to people. That was more challenging than just praying because He began to prompt me to carry very personal words of instruction or comfort to those needing it. For example, my husband and I were taking a defensive driving course to save on car insurance, and the class was full with people in diverse situations. Some were going through the class after a DUI; others were trying to regain their licenses after being incarcerated.

On our lunch break, we were conversing with others taking the class when God gave me specific instructions to carry a word to a certain man there. At first, I ignored the request, but I was strongly prompted again. I thought, *There's no way I can do that.* The man in question looked very intimidating, and I didn't know what to say to him. But the nudge was strong; I knew what had to be done. I trusted that I would know exactly what to say when I needed to. I had to take the first step. My heart was racing. He had his arms folded. He was standing tall like a bodyguard by the door, and he had a very serious demeanor.

My second challenge was asking to be excused from our lunch huddle. I said I had something important to do and would be right back. They watched me walk away with no

7

idea what I was doing. I hadn't told them what I was going to do. I was afraid that if I did, I would back down and the moment would be lost.

The man seemed much taller than I had first thought. I tapped his big shoulder and asked if he was open to hear a word I believed the Lord wanted me to carry to him. He softened his entire demeanor, unfolded his arms, and said, "Well yes. Sure. Go ahead." So at that point, I'm thinking, *Okay … What now?*

Normally, God would give me the word of knowledge and instruct me more clearly, and it would be more comfortable. Not that time. But then He revealed to me a vision of a young boy in his life, which prompted me to ask him if he had a son. I believe God does things like this in specific order to give more evidence that He is the one speaking through that person. The gentleman said, "Well yes, I have two sons." As soon as he told me that, God made it clear that the word of knowledge I was to share was that his son was desiring to spend more time with him.

After speaking this out and asking him if this meant anything, he replied, "I actually have been thinking that lately, and I know this is something I need to do." The look on his face when He felt the Lord's word come through me was beautiful.

When a word comes from the Lord, it is always one that should edify and lift a person rather than tear that person down. He thanked me, and we parted ways. This experience has helped me see that being obedient in the moment God prompts us can change the direction of someone's life if that person receives the word.

Chapter Two

Learning to Trust—
How God Showed Me

ONE NIGHT, I WAS LEAVING CLASS AND FELT THAT something was off in my spirit. I sat there before starting my car, and I smelled alcohol so strongly in my car that I wondered if someone was in the back seat waiting for me. I jumped out as fast as I could and looked in the back window. No one was there. I was safe.

I got back in and smelled the alcohol even more. I asked God, "What's going on?" My sister came to mind. She had been struggling with that addiction, and I realized I was to pray for her. I said a prayer for her to help her through whatever she was going through.

The next day, she told me that she had been without a drink for three days, that she was really struggling to break the cycle of drinking and had almost lapsed. Chills went down my spine. I began to see how the power of prayer could change someone's course in life. I realized I had just interceded for someone in need through hearing and listening to God's prompting of smell and through His voice.

I thought that if I could help my sister in her time of need, how many more people could I help if I weren't so distracted and just kept my eyes, ears, and nose alert. I felt fulfillment as never before and even more so than any experiences in the company I had so much success in. That kind of joy comes and goes, but this was something to last a lifetime.

All our lives are intricately woven together. Just as each stitch matters in quilting, it matters how we choose to listen and live. When we are careless or miss a piece when quilting, we can end up with holes or loose threading that could change how the final piece looks and compromise its quality and longevity.

Have you ever looked back at a time in your life and thought, *If only I would have ...?* I learned in my newfound understanding of God that if I missed an opportunity to hear and pray, He would speak to me by bringing a thought or someone to mind multiple times. Even when we miss what He tells us, He will continue to work through us in other avenues.

God speaks to us in different ways; He attracts our attention perhaps through a song on the radio, a nature walk during which we see His beauty, or by something someone says to us. We may even hear a voice in our minds that we know is not ours as we could never have thought the things we are hearing. He will circle back and not let up when He is instructing, warning, or giving us a word for ourselves or others. The quality of a quilt would be compromised if we were to miss something; the same is true if we miss hearing God's voice.

God will guide and reframe how and what He needs us to know. To understand things entirely, we must first learn about God's intent to have relationship with us through His son. In

2 Corinthians 3:15–17 (NIV), we read, "Even to this day when Moses is read, a veil covers their hearts. But whenever anyone turns to the Lord, the veil is taken away. Now the Lord is the Spirit, and where the Spirit of the Lord is, there is freedom." In this passage, Paul was saying that the only way the veil of separation between human understanding and God's glory can be removed is when we turn to the Lord and believe and trust that Christ died in our place for the forgiveness of our sin and set us free once and for all. Sin holds the veil in place, but forgiveness of sin removes the veil so there is no more shame, guilt, or condemnation. Where the Spirit of the Lord is, there is freedom from the veil that keeps people from seeing God's glory. Our eyes can see more clearly what God needs us to see.

I was taught to fear the Lord, and I experienced a lot of shame and guilt for my sins big and small that hindered me from knowing who I was in Christ. I thought I had to perform before I could receive God's acceptance.

If we truly understand 2 Corinthians 3:15–17, we can step into God's grace and out of the religious world. If God is truly in it and we are living with the Spirit, Christ in us, we should be operating in our new power rather than being in bondage.

Many churches still operate under the law and do not teach the fullness of grace; as a result, they do not experience the goodness God intends. There is no more we have to do to gain God's approval or love, and there is now nothing separating us from Him. He sees us as perfect, righteous, and clean from all sin now and forever through Jesus,

> **There is no more we have to do to gain God's approval or love, and there is now nothing separating us from Him.**

and we now have direct access to God. We no longer have to have man intercede for us to have relationship with our creator. We get to experience a connected and loving relationship with Him as He intended right when we choose to.

We become new creations set free from bondage from our works, performance, and the law. We gain the ability through Christ in us to rise above and live lives free of sin if we accept this gift and choose to operate and navigate with Him as our strength. Romans 8:2 (NIV) says, "Because through Christ Jesus the law of the Spirit who gives life has set you free from the law of sin and death." Unfortunately, many people are unaware that we are empowered and strengthened by His grace to rise above our fleshly ways. In John 10:10 (NIV), Jesus said, "The thief comes only to steal, and kill and destroy; I have come that they may have life, and have it to the full."

> **Without the Spirit in us, we cannot see from a higher level, only as far as our minds will allow.**

When we transfer these scriptures from our head knowledge and receive them as God intended in our hearts, we begin to live above our human capacity. Without the Spirit in us, we cannot see from a higher level, only as far as our minds will allow. Only God can stretch and grow us so that we can see from a broader perspective all He has for us. This requires us to first trust in Him.

When we begin to learn the Word of God, He will help us interpret it through the lens of the Holy Spirit.

Some of us may need to start from scratch to help make things new again just as we would if our quilting or stitching was incorrect. If we don't create a quilt right in the area necessary, it will look messy there and detract from its overall beauty. Some may want to begin with a different fabric. Some may need to throw away what they started in order to get the best result. Matthew 9:16–17 (NIV) says,

> No one sews a patch of unshrunk cloth on an old garment, for the patch will pull away from the garment, making the tear worse. Neither do people pour new wine into old wineskins. If they do, the skins will burst; the wine will run out and the wineskins will be ruined. No, they pour new wine into new wineskins, and both are preserved.

This scripture says that we cannot live under the law when we live under grace. The two do not mix, and when we try to see ourselves as righteous by our own efforts, we cannot experience the life Christ died to set us free from. We will always fall short of God's glory and find it impossible to measure up to it. In the same way, considering the religious rules and requirements we have been taught, we may need to start fresh in reading the Bible and ask God to reveal the truth where we have been believing lies or misunderstanding what we have learned from man and traditions alone.

As we go deeper into our relationship with God and get to know Him in the Spirit through the baptism of the Holy Spirit, we gain greater knowledge of what He has for us. Aligning with our specific purposes in life is better than anything we could do for ourselves, but we first have to call on him and seek His will. Jeremiah 29:11–13 says,

> **For I know the plans I have for you, declares the Lord, plans to prosper you and not to harm you, plans to give you a hope and a future. Then you will call on me and come and pray to me, and I will listen to you. You will seek me and find me when you seek me with all of your heart.**

Once we start seeking and calling out to Him, He will reveal things to us and bring us contacts, ideas, and influences and so much more than we could ever receive or do on our own. He will restore health and relationships and provide for us in ways we never could have imagined. In Ephesians 1:3, He promised and blessed us through Christ with every spiritual blessing in the heavenly realm, and He does not withhold one good thing from us. It is up to us to activate all God has for us on earth. Jeremiah 33:3 (NIV) says, "Call to Me, and I will answer you, and show you great and mighty things, which you do not know."

Many of us were taught about baptism or have witnessed baptisms of babies and adults. Baptizing a baby is the parents' choice to dedicate the life of the child to the Lord. Baptism as a youth or an adult is the personal choice to make a commitment to the Lord and profess one's faith as a testimony to all.

Many of us don't hear or haven't been taught about the second baptism that follows the water baptism. Matthew 3:11 (NIV) reads, "I baptize you with water for repentance. But after me comes one who is more powerful than I, whose sandals I am not worthy to carry. He will baptize you with the Holy Spirit and fire." This second baptism is the missing link for many churches to experience the flow and fullness of God's Spirit along with the evidence of the fruit that comes as a result of the Holy Spirit in action. Many don't experience miracles, healing, provision, or abundant lives because they are uneducated about the Holy Spirit's role or believe it was only for the disciples and leaders when Jesus walked the earth and not for them until they get to heaven.

Wedding rings are the outward symbol of marriage, but the marriage certificate and covenant we make with God to make two lives one make it official. What activates and allows two people in marriage to experience the fullness of what God designed it to be is our daily personal choice to go deeper with God in the center and surrender our lives to one another. This brings more clarity to and understanding of what the second baptism is in that when we take the step of water baptism, it is only a symbol and commitment of something much more meaningful.

What comes after is much more powerful; scripture describes it as the Holy Spirit and fire. The Holy Spirit's anointing and presence comes on us once we surrender our lives, which allows us to live in unity and in a deeper relationship where we get to experience all God has in heaven down on earth. This is not for just some of us but for all who choose to activate what has already been given.

Years after my water baptism, I experienced the second baptism of the Holy Spirit. For me, it was not directly following my choice to become water baptized. I believe it was directly proportionate to what I was ready to receive and was seeking it. This happens at different times for everyone, but the point is that it is available for all to receive.

I was at church one Sunday, and the sermon was on the Holy Spirit and receiving the gift of speaking in tongues. At the end of the service, anyone who desired to be prayed for and was ready to receive was invited up. I came up front eager to receive prayer and expecting to go deeper with God. I stood in between two pastors who were praying in their inner prayer language to God over me. In that moment, it seemed as though time stood still; it was one of the most beautiful and moving experiences in addition to getting water baptized years before.

They told me to just relax and let the words of the Spirit flow out of my mouth. The only thing that came out of my mouth was the same, simple, one-sound utterance over and over. After the prayer, I was encouraged to open my mouth whenever I could that week and allow the Lord to speak in and through me, and I did.

For the first week or so, it was just a simple sound that I repeated, but as I relied on the Holy Spirit, began to relax, and tuned my mind out, it began to blossom into so much more. I didn't receive the gift to interpret what my inner prayer language meant until several months later.

Everyone receives the Holy Spirit differently. If you are ready to go deeper and wish to receive this gift, my advice is to not overthink it, practice being still, and rid the distractions of life when you commune with God. Your mind will never make sense of this prayer language, but the Holy Spirit will give you an inner peace and the knowledge to understand when you let the Spirit lead you.

After I received the baptism of the Holy Spirit, I began

to see the power I had to heal disease, speak life into others, and reveal words of knowledge to people allowing them to recognize God was present all through Christ, who was living in me. I realized that the plan for my life was greater than myself. I began to see my life and the assignments God purposed for me that only I could fulfill. Through this book, I pray I can help you discover more about who God says you are and what He has available for you.

As stated earlier, Ephesians 1:3 (NIV) says, "Praise be to the God and Father of our Lord Jesus Christ, who has blessed us in the heavenly realms with every spiritual blessing in Christ." We have been given every spiritual blessing in Christ and have access to all He is with Him operating in and through us. He gives us power and strength to do all He did and even more on earth.

In 1 Corinthians 12:7–11 (NIV), we read,

> Now to each one the manifestation of Spirit is given for the common good. To one there is given through the Spirit a message of wisdom, to another a message of knowledge by means of the same Spirit, to another faith by the same Spirit, to another gifts of healing by that one Spirit, to another miraculous powers, to another prophecy, to another distinguishing between spirits, to another speaking in different kinds of tongues, and still to another the interpretation of tongues. All these are the work of one and the same Spirit, and he distributes them to each one, just as he determines.

When we grasp what we have already been given and are ready to go deeper with the Lord, He will make known to us things we have not seen.

When we grasp what we have already been given and are ready to go deeper with the Lord, He will make known to us things we have not seen. This includes our special gifts ready to be used. By our faith, God is able to unleash our best life.

Chapter Three

Transformation— Truth Revealed

AVE YOU EVER WATCHED THE TRANSFORMATION OF A butterfly from beginning to end, from cocoon to its final form? The most important stage is when the butterfly breaks out of its shell. It must do this on its own or it will die. Just like butterflies, we must go through some difficult stages before we can transform into the image Christ intended us to look like.

We are all going through our own walks; God is always at work in us if we have accepted Jesus into our hearts, and He is constantly pruning away whatever is not good for us. John 15:2 (NIV) says, "He cuts off every branch in me that bears no fruit, while every branch that does bear fruit he prunes so that it will be even more fruitful."

The beautiful thing about God is that He's constantly working things out for our good so that He can transform us once we let Him. When we let go and let Him get to work in and through us, we can come out of the dark place just like butterflies in their cocoons come into the light.

We have to activate our faith and take the steps necessary to break out of our old habits, our cocoons, and allow Him to help us change. When our obedience aligns with His will, we will transform into the beautiful person God wants to use for His glory in the kingdom. Activation comes into our lives when we acknowledge Him and where He wants to take us.

Praising Him for what He has done and will do in our lives will keep us focused on God rather than on ourselves or others. Psalm 139:13–14 (NIV) says, "For you created me in my inmost being; you knit me together in my mother's womb. I praise you because I am fearfully and wonderfully made; your works are wonderful, I know that full well."

You are a well-thought-out creation with a purpose far greater than you can imagine. He does not make mistakes; He would not know the most intimate details of your being without having a specific design just for you. He knows everything about your life—what you will do, who He will entrust to your care, what talents you possess, and more. He prepared for you to have more than enough even before your life began, and He is always working on your behalf. He has and is protecting you from harm and does not cause harm, pain, or anything else that would tear you down such as disease just to teach you a lesson. He watches over you even when you are in your

> He has and is protecting you from harm and does not cause harm, pain, or anything else that would tear you down such as disease just to teach you a lesson.

darkest hours, your darkest cocoon. You are forever anointed with the oil of Jesus and will never run out of favor, provision, health, love, and safety or lack anything.

When you know Him for who He truly is, you will know that your cup is overflowing with goodness all the days of your life. Psalm 23:5–6 (NIV) says, "You prepare a table before me in the presence of my enemies. You anoint my head with oil; my cup overflows. Surely your goodness and love will follow me all the days of my life."

The enemy knows this, and one of the greatest tactics he will use against you is lying to you. Satan will lie about whose you are and what power lies in you as a child of God. He works overtime distracting and clouding truth so that our lives in Christ are not even reality. You must be aware of his veil of lies meant to completely take you down.

Jesus rose victoriously from the grave so that we wouldn't have to wait to experience His goodness (Matthew 27:51). He did this so we could have direct access to our Father in heaven here on earth and for eternity. Jesus is the way, the truth, and the light. He defeated the enemy forever and gave us authority over the enemy to call out how our lives are to be. Luke 10:18–19 (NIV) reads, "I saw Satan fall like lightning from heaven. I have given you authority to trample on snakes and scorpions and to overcome all the power of the enemy; nothing will harm you."

Knowledge gives power, and this news transformed my life probably the most once I got it. I had new understanding of my authority on earth, and I began to take control over what I spoke and became more aware of the schemes of the enemy. I learned quickly that what my tongue spoke became reality. Proverbs 18:21 (NIV) says, "The tongue has the power of life and death, and those who love it will eat its fruit."

> What we speak can bring life or death into our situations. I began to speak against sickness and pain when it would come to me or others.

What we speak can bring life or death into our situations. I began to speak against sickness and pain when it would come to me or others. I began to claim provision for my career and for what I wanted for my husband and children. I spoke against any attacks we were facing, and I saw the power of Christ working through me. This is when the enemy has to flee. We experience the attacks and schemes of the devil only when we allow them. The devil requires a host. In Matthew 8:28–32, Jesus cast the enemy out of two men, and the evil spirits went into pigs. When we send the enemy away and no longer host him in our minds and lives, there will be no room for his evil works.

What do you need to begin speaking out in your life today? What in your health, marriage, finances, or future has the enemy been stealing from you? You are more than a conqueror in Jesus; He is with you to guide you to your best life. No more giving the enemy power and authority over your life. Take it back!

Chapter Four

Stepping into Greatness

J OHN 14:26–27 (NIV) READS,

> But the advocate, the Holy Spirit, whom
> the Father will send in My name, will
> teach you all things and will remind you
> of everything I have said to you. Peace I
> leave with you; my peace I give you. I do
> not give as the world gives. Do not let your
> hearts be troubled and do not be afraid.

You have the creator on your side guiding and teaching you daily. Learning to trust and give up all control to the Lord is very difficult. I am a very structured planner who likes to determine what my future will look like. Allowing God to be the Lord over all areas of my life is a work in progress for me, but it is becoming much easier to recognize.

Our flesh wants to take control naturally, but when we

give all circumstances we are facing to Him, things will start going more smoothly, and He can take the weight off our shoulders. This is better than any effort I would give in my own strength. Romans 12:2 (NIV) says, "Do not conform to the pattern of this world, but be transformed by the renewing of your mind. Then you will be able to test and approve what God's will is—his good, pleasing and perfect will." Learning that we no longer operate under the law but under grace has truly made me want to give my all to Him.

> **Our flesh wants to take control naturally, but when we give all circumstances we are facing to Him, things will start going more smoothly, and He can take the weight off our shoulders.**

God loves you beyond what you can comprehend; He knew that humankind would need a savior, so He sent His son to die for you so He would no longer be separated from you and His other children—all who put their faith in Jesus. He wants desperately to be with you for eternity.

This is not a forced relationship. He loves us just as parents love their children—unconditionally. No matter how their children choose to live, most parents love them the same. Unlike the Lord, people can mistreat you, and that can really mess with your mind about how you see God in your life.

> **Unlike the Lord, people can mistreat you, and that can really mess with your mind about how you see God in your life.**

If we have had an unhealthy family upbringing, one in which

love was conditional on our behavior, or if things happened that were simply out of our control, we can carry this weight into our relationships with others and how we relate to God.

Throughout most of my childhood and into my adult years, I lived in fear and let fear take over. I felt that if I didn't perform or please others, I would be rejected. I found myself accommodating, adjusting, and compromising who I was to please others and feel loved. I became a slave to what others wanted of me to the point that I did not know who I was, what true love was, and how God saw me. He began to show me in small but mighty ways that this was not truth. It was a pivotal moment in my life when He said through a leader to me, "Just because people don't agree with you or see things in a similar way doesn't mean they cannot still love you." I wondered that if that was true and I had been believing otherwise, how many more lies had I been believing in place of truth.

God finally had my attention, and I began to pray and ask Him about how He saw my life. When I opened my heart to Him and asked Him to show me His perspective, things were downloaded so clearly to me. Proverbs 19:20–21 (NIV) says, "Listen to advice and accept discipline and at the end you will be counted among the wise. Many are the plans in a person's heart, but it is the Lord's purpose that prevails."

It took years for me to become humble and submit to God. It was not due to pressure from people or even God; the overflow of God's love and grace for me opened my heart to want to give back to God just as children want to do their best for their parents because they feel the love and goodness in their hearts.

Bringing God my personal best has required me to redirect my focus to Him rather than to the world. When I live my life for my flesh—my selfish needs—or for the things that are not in His will for me, I feel lifeless, as if I had hit a wall after the temporary self-gratification wears off.

> Bringing God my personal best has required me to redirect my focus to Him rather than to the world.

If we choose what God has for us and follow His commands for us, we will experience complete joy and peace. Romans 8:6 (NIV) says, "The mind governed by the flesh is death, but the mind governed by the spirit if life and peace." I have had to learn that God has my best interests in mind in every area of my life, not just in certain ones. Learning to trust Him is the biggest faith walk in my life.

Here are some truths I have found while seeking His true nature and intent for His children. God wants you well, whole, healed, in good relationships, in life-giving marriages, with abundance in finances, and not living in depression or fear. Ask Him to show you His love for you and for a glimpse of how He wants your life to be. Then seek knowledge and wisdom in the Bible.

People will always give you their opinions and viewpoints and encourage or sway you in different ways. Learn to take everything to the Lord and ask Him, "Does this line up with what you want for me to do, act, or respond? What lies do I need to get rid of and replace with truth?"

Chapter Five

Knowing Who You Are

WHEN I BEGAN TO LEARN THE WORD AND WHAT GOD wanted for His children, I saw my worth in and through Him more clearly. I was able to shed the lies that religion had taught me. It was a beautiful thing.

> You are not what or who others say you are or what your circumstances are.

You are not what or who others say you are or what your circumstances are. You are royalty, and you have an inheritance that God clothes you in once you give your life to the Lord. Christ's blood becomes your precious covering. He washes away your sin and clothes you in His garments of salvation. You will become the righteousness of Christ. Isaiah 61:10 (NIV) says, "I will greatly rejoice in the Lord and my soul shall exult in my God, for He has clothed me with the garments of salvation; he has covered me with the robe of righteousness."

I had been looking to family and relationships as my source of joy when all along I had possessed a new identity so much greater in Christ. Christ will adopt us and give us grace, redemption, and forgiveness, and our identity will become the reflection of God. Ephesians 1:5–9 (NIV) says,

> **In love he predestined us for adoption to himself as sons through Jesus Christ, according to the purpose of his will to the praise of his glorious grace, with which he has blessed us in the Beloved. In him we have redemption through his blood, the forgiveness of our trespasses, according to the riches of his grace, which is lavished upon us, in all wisdom and insight and making known to us the mystery of his will according to his purpose, which he set forth in Christ.**

We don't have to depend on those around us to understand His plan for our lives and learn who we were called to be.

It's time for us to look to Him for all our needs and for the truth He has for us and who He says we are. This scripture clearly says that He will make known to us the mystery of His will. We don't have to depend on those around us to understand His plan for our lives and learn who we were called to be. How freeing it is when we understand this in our hearts. We are not under man's authority but God's.

We possess an everlasting inheritance for eternity. We are coheirs to the throne, more than a conqueror, and we are equipped to do even more than Jesus did on earth. This is the truth and hope

> **We are not under man's authority but God's.**

of where our identity lies. Ephesians 1:13–14 (NIV) says, "In him you also, when you heard the word of truth, the gospel of salvation, and believed in him and were sealed with the promised Holy Spirit, who is the guarantee of our inheritance until we acquire possession of it, to the praise of his glory." We

> **The gift of the Holy Spirit in us is our guide prompting and instructing us in the way we should go; the Holy Spirit helps us see our true identity and activates our inheritance on earth.**

will take possession of it once in heaven, but we already have possession of all God has for us on earth, and He wants us to take full advantage of the abundant life. The gift of the Holy Spirit in us is our guide prompting and instructing us in the way we should go; the Holy Spirit helps us see our true identity and activates our inheritance on earth.

In 3 John 1:2–4 (NIV), we read,

> Dear friend, I pray that you may enjoy good health and that all may go well for you, even as your soul is getting along well. It gave me great joy when some

believers came and testified about your faithfulness to the truth, telling how you continue to walk in it. I have no greater joy than to hear that my children are walking in the truth.

The NKJV version of that passage states that we will prosper in all things including our health.

These scriptures reveal that the truth is already in us. It's up to us to ask God to open our eyes to see our identity for what He already says the truth about us is. This scripture tells us that we are to prosper in all things. When we live out what He has called for us, that brings God great joy. Our heath, the wellness of our minds and souls, our finances, and our prosperity matter to God. We are to prosper in all things as children of God, not just in certain areas of life.

We are not defined by our situation, our sicknesses or diseases, our mental health, or our finances and relationships. Christ living in us gives us a new identity. Hebrews 1:3 (NIV) says, "The Son is the radiance of Gods glory and the exact representation of his being, sustaining all things by his powerful word." This describes our new identity in that we were created in the radiance of God's glory and in the exact representation of God himself. Wow! Super powerful when we grasp this and hard for the human mind to comprehend, but this is the truth about who we are.

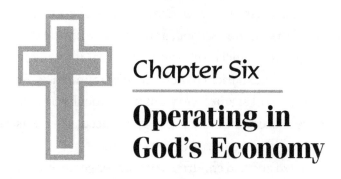

Chapter Six

Operating in God's Economy

DEUTERONOMY 28:12 (NIV) SAYS, "THE LORD WILL OPEN for you His good treasure house, the heavens, to give rain to your land in its season and to bless all the work of your hand and you will lend too many nations, but you will not borrow." The way the world teaches us to manage our money is not the way the spiritual economy works.

The United States has contributed to our financial priorities becoming out of alignment with how God intended. We are encouraged to spend beyond our limits and buy the next best things for the wrong reasons. To build our credit scores, we are told to expand our credit and debts rather than saving or investing. Many Americans live paycheck to paycheck and do not have enough to meet even the essentials such as health care and food. However, God has already laid out a plan for us to help us gain more knowledge and understanding of how we can operate in His economy.

I chose to go to college to better my future and avoid the downward spiral I had seen growing up, but when I graduated, I was in debt that I could not handle on my teacher's salary. I began a side business that was firmly established in the principles of God first, family second, and career third, and that began to change my financial situation. I felt that if I worked hard enough, I could experience increase and abundance. As great as that felt, it still seemed very empty to me. I was able to buy and have more than I had ever experienced, but I was exhausted and was feeling pressure to perform.

When I married and had children, I was no longer teaching, and my business took off. I put my career in the most important position until God moved me and my family to South Carolina. During that time, God began to show me that my priorities were out of alignment. I started to see my life differently and began to see that God's way was different from how I had been living. He wanted me to let go of myself and my own efforts and begin to trust in Him for my finances.

One of the hardest things God ever told me was that if I gave Him my business, everything would become easy. When He told me that, I was halfway to a national level and my team had a lot of momentum. I was being called to an unfamiliar place, and it was difficult to go there; it was not what I had seen or thought about for my future.

The Lord made it clear that I was being called to become a pastor. I was scared to death

> It wasn't that God wanted me to be lazy or not be successful; He wanted me to see what success and abundance looked like in the kingdom versus what it looked like in the world.

and resistant at first, but I knew that I needed to follow His calling and that somehow it would be better than my plans for myself. As I began to listen, I struggled with letting go of what I thought was normal in putting forth my efforts to earn money. It wasn't that God wanted me to be lazy or not be successful; He wanted me to see what success and abundance looked like in the kingdom versus what it looked like in the world. I trusted God with my finances and how I should manage what He provided me; that was a challenge, but I learned to face it.

For a time, I needed to pull back from my business and focus on becoming ordained. That was a huge faith walk in that I took three years off from working full time. What I had built for over fifteen years took a back seat. I had monthly quotas, and I had to continue to trust God to provide when I wasn't working. Many times and even now, I listen to His instruction and ask myself, *How will I ever be able to make what I need if I don't put the effort in?* But just when I consider something impossible, He provides in ways I could never have imagined.

One time, I had an oral procedure done and thought, *I hope I have enough to pay for this without dental insurance.* I had received an estimate for the oral surgery and thought I would have to pay hundreds, but the receptionist later told me that the surgeon had said there would be no charge that day. It was not by chance that that happened; it was the Lord's prompting the surgeon, who listened to Him. I wept and almost fell to my knees just before getting into my car after I had heard that, and I thanked God for always providing for my needs. Many times before that, I had experienced similar situations, but in that moment, I chose to surrender all worry and doubt to God and trust Him with my finances.

Sowing His seeds and building in the areas He leads me to has become a focus for me and where I have been able to experience great changes in my life. I have learned to ask God to show me to whom, what, and where my finances should go specifically, not just where I pleased or felt led. It can be easy at times to slip into the old ways, and when I try to be my main resource, things fall apart. I have learned that putting my life, business, and finances in His hands leads me to streams of living water.

> In God's economy and cycle of life, there is a constant flow with an abundance of resources always at our fingertips, and they will never run out!

What does it mean to sow His seed or to sow into the kingdom? Why is that important? In God's economy and cycle of life, there is a constant flow with an abundance of resources always at our fingertips, and they will never run out! Isaiah 55:10–11 (NIV) tells us,

> As the rain and the snow come down from heaven, and do not return to it without watering the earth and making it bud and flourish, so that it yields seed for the sower and bread for the eater, so is my word that goes out from my mouth: It will not return to me empty, but will accomplish what I desire and achieve the purpose for which I sent it.

The Amplified version of the Bible says, "It will not return to Me void (useless without result)." God always provides results for us with His unlimited resources. His goodness to us prompts us to respond with the overflow of our hearts, give our best back to the Lord, and provide for those in need in the kingdom.

God does not force us to give back, to sow seed to others, but it is a beautiful way we can honor Him. The world has put a religious stigma on what it means to give. This is to be done in private; God knows the intention of our hearts. Giving is between us and God, not between us and anyone else,

> **His goodness to us prompts us to respond with the overflow of our hearts, give our best back to the Lord, and provide for those in need in the kingdom.**

even the church. Deuteronomy 28:12 reads, "You will lend to many nations but will borrow from none." The next verse reads, "The Lord will make you the head, not the tail. If you pay attention to the commands of the Lord your God that I give you this day and carefully follow them, you will always be at the top, never at the bottom."

The problem is our lack of knowledge about what is available to us through Christ. If we follow His commands, we will thrive as He created us to. His ways are always higher and lead to life. We have to retrain our brains to grasp God's promises. We are not in a place of lack! We must not follow the ways of the

> **We have to retrain our brains to grasp God's promises.**

world and idolize people or possessions; that is putting the gods of the world before our Lord in heaven.

In the beginning of time, God gave us all He had that was good and withheld nothing (Genesis 2:8–9). Genesis 2:15

(NIV) states, "The Lord God took the man and put him in the Garden of Eden to work it and take care of it. And the Lord God commanded the man, You are free to eat from any tree in the garden."

We were made to have every good thing in abundance from the beginning. When we try to take matters into our own hands and think we are the reason we have all we have earned, we can hurt ourselves and change the course of our prosperity. We begin to even sometimes play God over our lives at times due to greed and thinking our ways are better, which is exactly what humanity did in the beginning of time. Humans accused God of withholding something good, tested Him, and became greedy even though they had had it all given to them already.

God gave us specific instruction to protect us after giving us an abundance in Genesis 2:17 (NIV): "But you must not eat from the tree of the knowledge of good and evil, for when you eat from it you will certainly die." The most important thing we miss as children of God is that we don't understand that God first loved us and that He wanted us to experience lives of joy and blessings. Humanity was deceived by the enemy and fell. Genesis 3:4–6 (NIV) reads, "You will certainly die, the serpent said to the woman. For God knows that when you eat from it your eyes will be opened, and you will be like God, knowing good and evil." We chose not to listen to the very thing that was meant to protect us from the ways of evil. The enemy's job is to kill, steal, and destroy us by deceiving us into thinking that God is withholding something good from us. That is the real problem we face. Humanity was responsible for Satan's being given power in the world, which is why there is sin, disease, pain, and suffering. We sabotaged our inheritance from God. That was the moment God was saddened by His creation and had to remove the gifting of all He had given that was meant to bless us. Genesis 3:23 (NIV) says, "So the Lord God banished him from the Garden of Eden to work the ground from which he had been taken." Humanity rejected what God meant to bless it with, and by this act of disobedience, God knew He had to have a better plan for His children.

God was protecting us a second time in Genesis 3:24 (NIV): "After he drove the man out, he placed on the east side of the Garden of Eden cherubim and a flaming sword flashing back and forth to guard the way to the tree of life." Had Adam and Eve obeyed God, they could have lived there forever. After disobeying, Adam and Eve no longer deserved paradise, and God told them to leave. In Genesis 3:24, God again was not rejecting them or withholding the good by making them leave; He was protecting them again. If they had continued to live in the garden and had eaten from the Tree of Life, they would have lived forever in their sinful nature, and that would have meant an eternity of living apart from God and continually trying to hide for the rest their lives.

God loves us so much; He knew He had to prepare a different way through the sacrifice of His son, Jesus Christ, in exchange for our sin so we could have a way to live with Him for eternity in heaven. Christ's death is the bridge for us back to the garden not just here on earth but also for eternity. We no longer have to be separated from God and the blessings He originally had in store for us. On earth, we have a new kingdom way, and there is nothing we don't already possess in and through Christ or is being withheld. It is truly at our fingertips. The hardest part is having the faith to accept all He has for us as our new truth. He didn't send His son to die a horrific death so that we would have a life that was less than what it could have been.

> It is up to us to have faith that we can have all God initially promised we could have and know that what we ask for and claim as our inheritance is already ours through Christ in us.

It's time to open our eyes and grab all He has for us on earth. It is up to us to have faith that we can have all God initially promised we could have and know that what we ask for and claim as our inheritance is already ours through Christ in us. Psalm 2:8 (NIV) states, "Ask me, and I will make nations your inheritance, the ends of the earth your possession." Hebrews 1:2 (NIV) says, "But in these last days he has spoken to us by his Son, whom he appointed heir of all things, and through whom also he made the universe." Matthew 28:18 (NIV) says, "Then Jesus came to them and said, All authority in heaven and on earth has been given to me."

Chapter Seven

Drowning Out the Negative Noise of the World

ADVERSITIES AND NEGATIVITY WILL COME TO US THROUGH people, the news, social media, and other outside sources, but Jesus told us to expect them and consider it pure joy when we go through these adversities because they will cause perseverance, completeness, and maturity in our faith. James 1:2–4 (NIV) says,

> Consider it pure joy, my brothers and sisters, whenever you face trial of many kinds, because you know that the testing of your faith produces perseverance. Let perseverance finish its work so that you may be mature and complete, not lacking anything.

When I was going through one of my most difficult times, I read that passage and God told me, "The trials of this world are minute compared to that of those souls who will not be with me in eternity." This word and scripture helped me reframe my mindset in the midst of the negative noise of the world constantly coming in and all around me.

When I was young, I was a people pleaser and lived for years for what others wanted and needed from me. But over time, by discerning God's wisdom, I learned that those who had no love for

> "The trials of this world are minute compared to that of those souls who will not be with me in eternity."

themselves and allowed others to dictate who they were were guilty of sinning as much as were those who were boastful, filled with pride, and lived for self. In both cases, the people on either end of that spectrum were serving themselves or others before God. There are no greater commandments the Lord gave us than to love God over self (Mark 12:30) and to love our neighbors as ourselves (Mark 12:31), which means we must love ourselves.

Proverbs 3:6 NIV reads, "In all your ways submit to him, and he will make your paths straight." I saw this reality unfolding in my life in that I was always following others'

> If we live for man, we will not accomplish His will or serve the purpose He has designed for us.

lead rather than God's. It was life changing for me to recognize this was happening and break free of man's control.

God places and uses key people in our lives to help build His kingdom, so it is critical that we allow others to speak into our lives.

Ultimately, it is Him we need to trust and obey. If we live for man, we will not accomplish His will or serve the purpose He has designed for us. This is like a water hose with a kink that stops the flow of water and does not allow it to serve its purpose. The same is true of the Holy Spirit becoming blocked and unable to flow in and through us in the way God intended or purposed for our lives. When we put others before our creator to be our guide, lives and souls are at stake.

> **When we put others before our creator to be our guide, lives and souls are at stake.**

God working in and through us can cause lives to be transformed in a massive way. Psalm 146:3–4 (NIV) says, "Do not put your trust in princes, in human beings, who cannot save. When their spirit departs, they return to the ground; on that very day their plans come to nothing." While it is important that we are teachable and can learn very valuable, life-changing lessons along with wisdom from our elders, peers, and leaders in and out of church, that should never be the main source driving our lives.

God was teaching me this lesson during one of the most difficult times in my life in that I felt physically isolated for a long time. I believe God knew I needed to retreat and withdraw from all leaders and great and not-so-great influences to break free from man's control over my life. We can better learn to trust,

> **Sometimes, we can be doing great things, serving others, leading in a church or at our jobs, but being out of alignment with God can hinder the plans and timing He has for us.**

41

hear, and discern God's plans for our lives more clearly after He removes what is comfortable and familiar from our lives. I had no one else to look to but God, who drowned out the noise of the world so that I could shift my thoughts and focus and get in alignment with Him. Sometimes, we can be doing great things, serving others, leading in a church or at our jobs, but being out of alignment with God can hinder the plans and timing He has for us.

In the process of metamorphosis from a caterpillar to a butterfly, the old body dies and a new body forms inside a protective shell, the chrysalis. This cocoon is built so that the caterpillar can safely rest and digest all the food it has consumed earlier. A dramatic transformation takes place in the cocoon. Just as this is a necessary step for a caterpillar to transform into a butterfly, we must also die to our old ways and the ways of the world to become the beautiful creations God intends us to be.

This time of solitude with God is also crucial for us to drown out the negative noise of the world and hear His voice. When we retreat from the world, we can take what we hear God say and make sure it aligns with what the Bible says. Sometimes, our thoughts and ways can become skewed, so it is important that the Bible becomes our guide and confirms what we hear God telling us.

Christ modeled that when He retreated to hear the Father's voice and discern and get confirmation that what He was hearing was accurate and truly the assignment the Father had specifically for Him. The timing of the Father's instruction was crucial as well. In Luke 6:12, we read that Jesus had to disconnect, go to the mountainside to pray, and spend the night praying to God. Matthew 26:39 (NIV) says, "Going a little farther, he fell with his face to the ground and prayed, My Father, if it is possible, may this cup be taken from me. Yet not as I will, but as you will."

This time of retreating or being in the cocoon can also be a time for us to renew our minds and break free from the control we and others have over our lives. This was modeled for us when Jesus said in the previous scripture, "Yet not as I will, but as you will." He was clearly overwhelmed in the physical with the assignment God had for Him, and He wrestled with what was to come, which is why He said, "Father if it is possible, may this cup be taken from me." The lesson in His obedience was that He had to align His will with God the Father, gain clarity, and let God work in and through Him to save the world.

What are we holding onto or have control over that we do not want to hand over to God? What plans of ours are not able to come to fruition as a result of our disobedience?

After a butterfly breaks free from its cocoon, its wings are folded and wet, and it needs to rest to allow blood to flow into its wings. Just as a butterfly needs to wait to take to flight, we need to set aside our personal agenda and timing and wait for God to help us soar when we are fully prepared. In 1 Corinthians 3:1–2 (NIV), we read,

> **Brothers and sisters, I could not address you as people who live by the Spirit but as people who are still worldly—merely infants in Christ. I gave you milk, not solid food, for you were not yet ready for it. Indeed you are still not ready. You are still worldly.**

43

We have to accept and thank God where we are sometimes and know that when we are in alignment with what He has for us and are willing to listen, the Holy Spirit can then flow in and through us more regularly without our even thinking about it.

We should learn to embrace the season He has us in and begin to see the preparation time in our lives as valuable and necessary so we can begin to soar relying on the Holy Spirit, Christ in us, to give us power and strength. This time in the cocoon and transformation is and will also be true when it is our time to pass on. We will leave our shells, our earthly bodies, and gain new, restored heavenly bodies and life with Christ for eternity. We will be made new, be free of all pain and suffering, be forever released from the heartaches of life on earth, and soar to a new level.

> **We should learn to embrace the season He has us in and begin to see the preparation time in our lives as valuable and necessary so we can begin to soar relying on the Holy Spirit, Christ in us, to give us power and strength.**

Chapter Eight

The Goodness of God

SALM 34:8–10 (NIV) SAYS, "TASTE AND SEE THAT THE Lord is good; blessed is the one who takes refuge in him. Fear the Lord, you his holy people, for those who fear him lack nothing. The lions may grow weak and hungry, but those who seek the Lord lack no good thing."

When I was young, I struggled to understand God's goodness. I feared the Lord and often felt condemned rather than empowered by His goodness. I often thought that there had to be more to God than just being scared to know Him.

Years later, when I began to seek God's true character and nature, I had to meditate and gain clarity from the Lord on what the word *fear* meant when used in reference to the Lord so many times in the Bible. God began to show me that the word meant knowledge of and wisdom in and confirmed this for me in *Strong's Concordance*. When you read the word *fear* in the Bible as in "fear the Lord," understand that it is not the negative meaning the world has made it out to be but rather the beginning of knowledge or wisdom of God's goodness.

Let's take a few examples from Proverbs and Psalms. Proverbs was written primarily for instruction on how to live abundantly as God intended. Psalms was written for thanking God and gleaning wisdom and knowledge of how to survive situations that befall us. These scriptures will show His goodness and true nature and not put the fear of God in our lives. When fear is instilled in us, our natural reaction is to push away and not want to be near anyone or anything causing us to fear.

Proverbs 19:23 (NIV) says, "The fear of the Lord leads to life; then one rests content, untouched by trouble." I gained clarity when I read it this way: "The wisdom of the Lord leads to life; then one rests content, untouched by trouble."

Psalm 25:12–14 (NIV) says,

> **Who, then, are those who fear the Lord? He will instruct them in the ways they should choose. They will spend their days in prosperity, and their descendants will inherit the land. The Lord confides in those who fear him; he makes his covenant known to them.**

I learned more about God's goodness when I read it this way.

> **Who, then are those who have wisdom in the Lord? He will instruct them in ways they should choose. They will spend their**

days in prosperity, and their descendants will inherit the land. The Lord confides in those who have knowledge of him; he makes his covenant known to them.

Imagine a child fearing his dad's reaction for doing something that could have really hurt him such as touching a stovetop. The love of the earthly father is in the knowledge or wisdom that his child could really get hurt for doing something like touching a hot stove; the father wants to protect his son. The same is true of our Father, who wants us to know His nature and have wisdom in His goodness for us.

Living a life without our creator is to be separated from the one who best knows, loves, and guides us and the lives we were meant to live. We are born with the innate ability to hear our creator's voice, but the world can affect our abilities to hear more clearly or at all. Even with the noises of the world all around us, God makes it plain to us. Romans 1:19–20 (NIV) tells us,

Since what may be known about God is plain to them, because God has made it plain to them. For since the creation of the world God's invisible qualities—his eternal power and divine nature—have been clearly seen, being understood from what has been made, so that people are without excuse.

When we search God and are ready to commune with Him, the clouds of confusion will lift and we will be able to discern the difference between our voices and His in our minds. At that point, the enemy will no longer have a hold on us or be able to keep us from hearing Him speak to us.

> **When we search God and are ready to commune with Him, the clouds of confusion will lift and we will be able to discern the difference between our voices and His in our minds.**

As our minds' gatekeepers, we can control what we let come into them. Some were never given a Bible or brought up with the knowledge of God, and some were raised in other belief systems, but God's Word still holds true—We were designed to have connection with Him and equipped to see clearly His eternal power and divine nature, so we are without excuse if we do not. God gives us free will to accept Him or deny His existence; He will never force the matter. His love for us is infinite and never changes.

God grieves for those He does not have relationship with. Matthew 18:12–14 (NIV) says,

> What do you think? If a man owns a hundred sheep, and one of them wanders away, will he not leave the ninety-nine on the hills and go to look for the one that wandered off? And if he finds it, truly I tell you, he is happier about that one sheep than about the ninety-nine that did not wander off. In the same way your Father in heaven is not willing that any of these little ones should perish.

He will forever be waiting for you with open arms and will

continue to show up in your life and desire a relationship with you right where you are.

We will all come to know our Father in heaven, and the world will acknowledge Him. Romans 14:11–12 (NIV) says, "It is written: As surely as I live, says the Lord, every knee will bow before me; every tongue will acknowledge God. So then, each of us will give an account of ourselves to God."

Chapter Nine

Forgiveness

IN THE PROCESS OF IDENTIFYING YOUR WORTH IN CHRIST, NOT through how others see you or how they have mistreated you, realize that forgiveness is crucial for you to experience God's grace and mercy fully. Unwillingness to forgive others or even God can block His goodness and blessings He has for you and wants to do through your life. In Mark 12:30–31, God asked us to first love Him with all our heart, soul, and mind and second to love our neighbors as we love ourselves. To understand why this is the most powerful and greatest commandment, we have to understand His mercy, grace, and the love and forgiveness He has shown us. The overflow of His goodness causes us to respond in love, which is our strength to forgive.

> **The overflow of His goodness causes us to respond in love, which is our strength to forgive.**

We will all have good and bad things happen to us, and we will find some things hard to let go of that can even become part of our identity. This is especially true when tragedy comes our way in the form of disease or the loss of a loved one.

One of the first steps to forgiving God is understanding that He is and will never be the cause of our pain. God calls us to health, wholeness, long life, and an abundance through His son, who made the ultimate sacrifice on our behalf. We often like to blame God to be able to have a means for justice and understanding when in actuality, there are so many other factors that are blocking blessings or causing us pain that we might not understand.

> **We often like to blame God to be able to have a means for justice and understanding when in actuality, there are so many other factors that are blocking blessings or causing us pain that we might not understand.**

I am hoping this will clarify that God is not the cause. We have free will; our actions matter, and sin or disobedience can change the course of our and others' lives and block blessings or opportunities that God specifically had for us or others to receive.

We have responsibility on earth, and people can be the direct cause of a negative outcome based on daily choices. After all, we handed over our authority to the enemy from the beginning of time; humankind opened up the forces of evil in the world—disease, famine, poverty, tragic accidents, addictions, and so much more. From the beginning, God wanted His children to have full lives without pain, suffering, or disease.

John 10:10 (NIV) says, "The thief comes only to steal and kill and destroy; I have come that they may have life, and have it to the full." The enemy's job is to kill or destroy, but the Bible clearly gives us instruction on how to handle the devil's schemes of the devil in our lives; 1 Peter 5:8 (NIV) says,

> Be alert and of sober mind. Your enemy the devil prowls around like a roaring lion looking for someone to devour. Resist him, standing firm in the faith, because you know that the family of believers throughout the world is undergoing the same kind of sufferings. And the God of all grace, who called you to his eternal glory in Christ, after you have suffered a little while, will himself restore you and make you strong, firm and steadfast. To him be the power forever and ever. Amen.

Once we are clear on the fact that God is not our enemy and does not control others, we can see that what happens in our lives is a direct result of our choices, the consequences of sin and disobedience, the decision others make around us good or bad, and last, the work of the devil.

Another step to forgiveness aside from knowing God is on our side and working on our behalf is getting rid of anger and malice. Anger is a natural feeling, one that even Jesus felt when He responded to those misusing the temple. But if we hold onto anger, that opens a door for the enemy to come in and take root. That puts a weight on us we were never meant to carry, and it can be cancerous to every area of our lives. Ephesians 4:31–32 NIV says, "Get rid of all bitterness, rage and anger, brawling and slander, along with every kind of malice. Be kind and compassionate to one another, forgiving each other, just as in Christ God forgave you."

When we truly see that we have new identity in Christ, that He died a horrific death to set us free for eternity, and that He forgives us fully even when we aren't worthy of forgiveness, we consider that pretty incredible. Imagine taking on the punishment for a friend or loved one and suffering the worst kind of pain to take the blame for something that that friend or loved one did. That is the ultimate form of love, and out of this great love comes the overflow of His pouring out on us and strengthening us to be able to forgive.

Another step of working through forgiveness is understanding that it can take time for a person to heal or it can happen in an instant. Sometimes, we have to get more clarity and wisdom about where we need to take responsibility versus what was completely out of our control. When we include God in our journey, He can help us navigate it by revealing specific points or behaviors that do not serve others and give instruction on how best to handle our journeys. Sometimes, He will even cut people out of our lives to protect us or give us the wisdom to do that ourselves. We must learn to set healthy boundaries and distance ourselves for a while from at times even those we are the closest to particularly if manipulation, control, abuse, or any other pain is involved.

We can sometimes create debts that people owe us when they don't measure up or treat us justly, but we cannot truly love others when we cast debts on them. This enslaves others to our control. This is true for ourselves and for those who mistreat us. Forgiveness is not for the person we hold in contempt but rather for ourselves so we can operate in the freedom God designed for us that allows us to enjoy lives full of peace.

Forgiveness is not for the person we hold in contempt but rather for ourselves so we can operate in the freedom God designed for us that allows us to enjoy lives full of peace.

We are all sinners and fall short and make mistakes; that is why we need a savior. It is important that we don't put our faith, hope, and expectations in others to define our identity. This will create dead ends and not be life giving to any relationship. God empowers us to rise above the sin when we shift our focus and bring our ways, thoughts, and actions before Him and ask for counsel. In 2 Corinthians 3:4–6 (NIV), we read,

> Such confidence we have through Christ before God. Not that we are competent in ourselves to claim anything for ourselves, but our competence comes from God. He has made us competent as ministers of a new covenant – not of the letter but of the Spirit; for the letter kills, but the Spirit gives life.

Putting rules or the law before others to follow will kill or not be life giving to our relationships, but living in His grace and showing mercy to others even when they sometimes don't deserve it will produce life. This is so important to take in and is ultimately the one thing that will let us out of bondage.

God strengthens us to show love and mercy to those who have wronged us, but that doesn't mean we have to be in agreement with the choices they have made and have them in our lives. It may be that permanent separation is necessary after seeking discernment about what is best for that specific relationship. Forgiveness can look different in each situation and does not always mean we need to be near those who have caused us pain.

To transform and allow room for forgiveness in our hearts, we must take responsibility for our thoughts and renew them daily in the Lord. Romans 12:2 (NIV) says, "Do not conform to the pattern of this world, but be transformed by the renewing of your mind. Then you will be able to test and approve what God's will is—his good, pleasing and perfect will."

Living in the flesh will pull us away from the Spirit's leading, our source of life and wholeness. This is a dangerous place to live, but when we renew our minds and submit our thoughts to God, Christ in us will give us strength and power to align with His mighty and perfect will and give us the greatest comfort and peace. By focusing our lives on the Word of God, we learn to see people and even those who hurt us deeply as Jesus sees them. He said, "Forgive them Father, for they know not what they do!"

Someday, maybe not until heaven, God will repay you for the unjust acts you have suffered. In 2 Thessalonians 1:6–7 (NIV) we read, "God is just: He will pay back trouble to those who trouble you and give relief to you who are troubled, and to us as well. This will happen when the Lord Jesus is revealed from heaven in blazing fire with his powerful angels."

The hardest step in letting go once and for all is learning our authority over the enemy and taking our power back through Christ. We must learn to rebuke the enemy when he tries to bring up lies about where our identity comes from. We can no longer be the host for the enemy to have control over. God's Word is true and doesn't shift like blowing sand. It remains the same yesterday, today, and forever. James 1:16–17 (NIV) says, "Don't be deceived, my dear brothers and sisters. Every good and perfect gift is from above, coming down from the Father of the heavenly lights, **who does not change like shifting shadows.**"

> **We can no longer be the host for the enemy to have control over.**

The Bible states that Christ rose victoriously over darkness and defeated Satan once and for all and that all power and authority has been given to us in the same way with Christ in us, therefore giving us the power to rebuke or speak against the enemy. Jesus said in Luke 10:18–19 (NIV), "I saw Satan fall like lightning from heaven. I have given you authority to trample on snakes and scorpions and to overcome all the power of the enemy; nothing will harm you."

> **The Bible states that Christ rose victoriously over darkness and defeated Satan once and for all and that all power and authority has been given to us in the same way with Christ in us, therefore giving us the power to rebuke or speak against the enemy.**

I mentioned earlier that the job of the enemy is to kill, steal, and destroy, so we cannot give him the upper hand. When situations or people rise up against us and we are feeling hopeless or defeated, we must remember who we are and learn to discard the lies the enemy will speak to us.

We are children of God and coheirs with Christ, who gives us the strength and power to overcome darkness. It is up to us to activate our authority on earth. Ephesians 3:19–20 (NIV) says,

> **And to know this love that surpasses knowledge—that you may be filled to the measure of all the fullness of God. Now to him who is able to do immeasurably more than all we ask or imagine, according to his power that is at work within us.**

About the Author

Joele S. Leith has been leading women professionally throughout her career for more than twenty years, helping them know their worth in Christ and understand their God-given potential. She is an ordained pastor who runs a church called Clothed in Righteousness. She and her husband, David, have two children and live in Michigan.

CPSIA information can be obtained
at www.ICGtesting.com
Printed in the USA
BVHW030233250121
598665BV00011B/406

9 781664 211278